And here's what you do!

1 Copy each step-by-step drawing onto your grid paper, noticing where the drawing should touch the lines on your grid. Draw lightly in pencil. Since each new step is shown in blue, you'll always know exactly what to do next.

TIP: Be sure to start in the middle of the grid paper.

2 You may erase the pencil construction lines as you go along so that you can see how your drawing is progressing. When you have finished, use your felt-tip pen to go over the lines you want to keep, and erase any stray pencil lines.

Now you have a perfect drawing to color any way you'd like! Before you color, you may want to read pages 30 - 32 for some extra coloring tips.

Ladybug

Draw a circle for the shell and add a head and six legs. Divide the shell with a curved line.

1

Add spots, antennae, and details on the legs.

2

3

Use your felt-tip pen to trace over the lines you want to keep, and erase any stray pencil lines.

4 Color your ladybug!

4

I Can DRAW Everything

Cover illustrated by Renée Daily

Interiors illustrated by Yuri Salzman, Mary Grace Eubank, Len Epstein, and George Gaadt

Here's what you need...

You're about to become an artist! Before you start, make sure you have a pencil, a pencil sharpener, an eraser, a felt-tip pen, and one or more of the different coloring media pictured here. Then, look in the back of the book for your grid pages. They'll help you to follow the special drawing steps. If you need more paper, you can ask a grownup to help you to copy them.

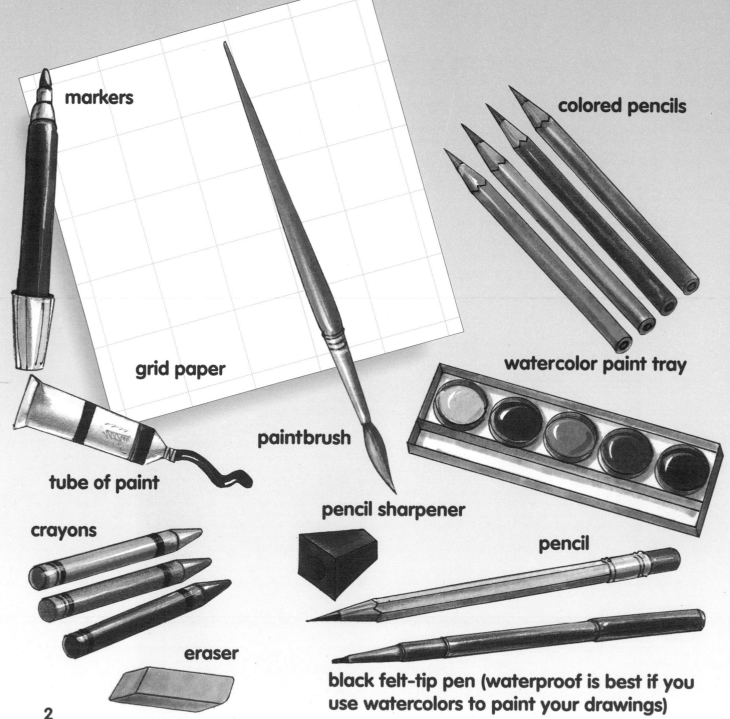

markers

colored pencils

grid paper

watercolor paint tray

paintbrush

tube of paint

pencil sharpener

crayons

pencil

eraser

black felt-tip pen (waterproof is best if you use watercolors to paint your drawings)

2

Jimmy Giraffe

Add details to the head and body and dress your giraffe in a turtleneck sweater. Draw a twig in its mouth.

Draw the head, neck, body, and legs. Add two small circles at the top of the head for eyes.

1

2

Use your felt-tip pen to trace over the lines you want to keep, and erase the extra pencil lines.

3

4 Color your giraffe!

Indy Car

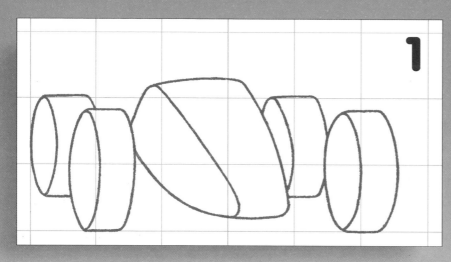

1 Draw a wedge shape for the body and add four wheels on the sides.

Draw the rear wing, the cockpit for the driver, and add lines to connect the body to the wheels.

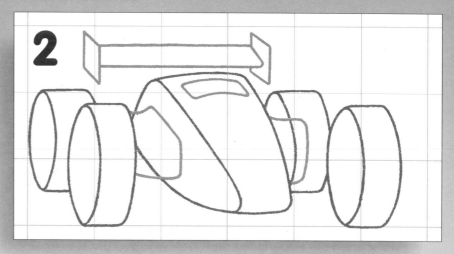

2

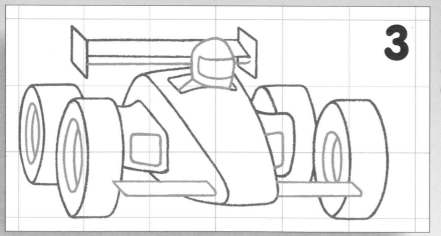

3 Draw the front wing, side pod details, wheel ovals, and the driver's helmet and shoulder.

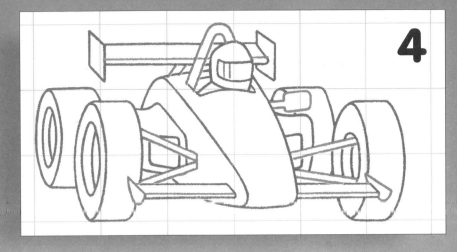

4 Draw suspension struts to connect the wheels to the body. Add details to the helmet and the front and rear wings. Draw a side-view mirror, and add a roll bar behind the driver.

Use your felt tip pen to trace the lines you want to keep, and erase the extra pencil lines.

5

6 Color your Indy car!

Bee

Keep your pencil sharp and draw lightly for the best results.

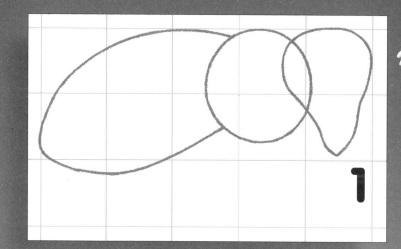

1 Draw a circle for the thorax, and add a long abdomen on one side and a pear-shaped. head on the other.

Add the five visible legs, antennae segments, and details on the head and mandible.

2

3 Finish the antennae and draw two long, curved wings. Give your bee large eyes and divide the legs into segments.

8

4 Add stripes on the abdomen, four small feelers, and details on the legs, head, and antennae to complete your drawing.

Use your felt-tip pen to trace over the lines you want to keep, and erase any stray pencil lines.

5

6 Color your bee!

Raccoon

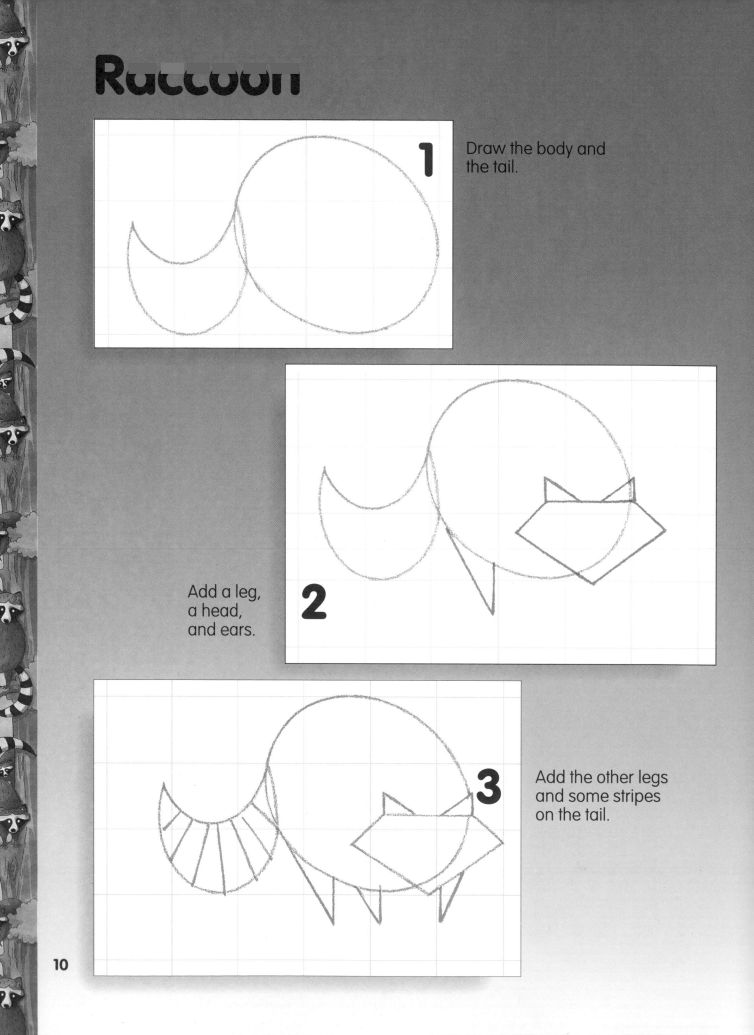

1 Draw the body and the tail.

2 Add a leg, a head, and ears.

3 Add the other legs and some stripes on the tail.

10

Draw curved lines on the face. Then add eyes, whiskers, and the raccoon's mask and paws.

4

5 Use your felt-tip pen to trace over the lines you want to keep, and erase the extra pencil lines.

6 Color your raccoon!

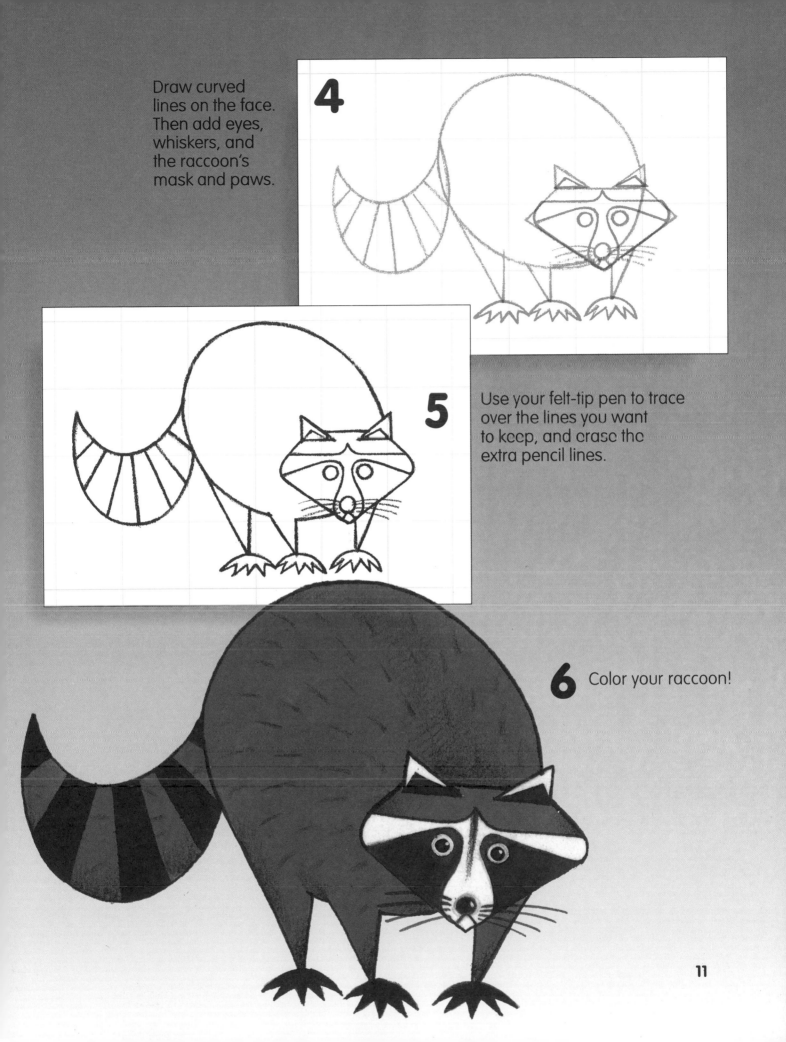

Super Hero

Draw a large, round, upper body and smaller, overlapping head.

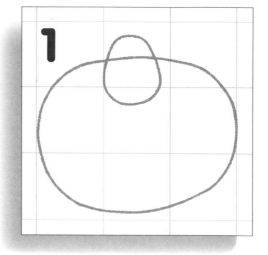

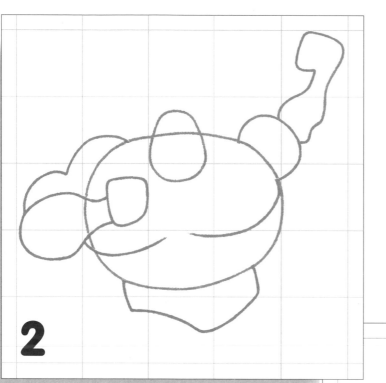

Use rounded shapes and curved lines to draw the arms and hands, the muscles on the chest, and the shorts.

Define the fingers and add details to the head and body. Draw the rounded legs.

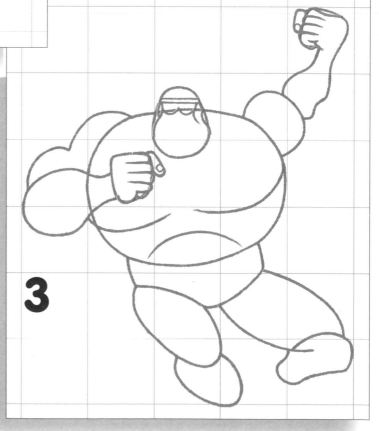

4 Finish your drawing with a face, a helmet, boots, a cape, and more details on the costume belt and buckle.

Use your felt-tip pen to trace over the lines you want to keep, and erase any stray pencil lines.

5

6 Color your Super Hero!

Itty Bitty Kitty

Draw a circle for the head and an overlapping oval for the body. Add smaller curved shapes for front and back legs.

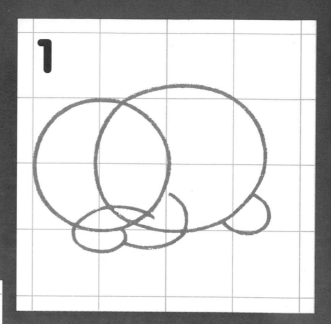

Draw another front leg, eyes, a nose, and a mouth.

Give your cat pointed ears and a curved tail and add more definition to the top of the head. Draw a small circle and oval to make the bird's head and body.

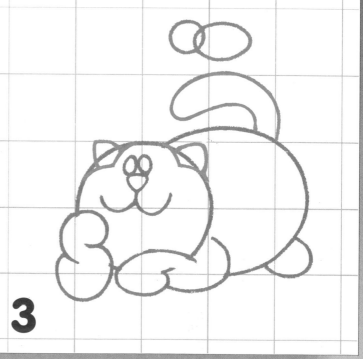

4

Draw the toes and eye pupils and add details to the ears and face. Complete your cat with rough outlines to show fur. Finish the bird with a wing, eyes, a beak, legs, and a tail.

5

Use your felt-tip pen to trace over the lines you want to keep, and erase the extra pencil lines.

6 Color your cat!

Stegosaurus

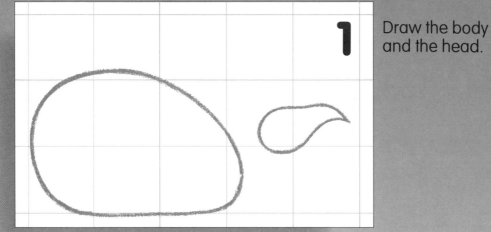

1 Draw the body and the head.

2 Draw ovals for the neck and the tops of the legs. Use curved lines for the tail.

3 Add pointed plates down your Stegosaurus' back, tail, and neck. Draw a mouth and an eye, and finish the legs.

4 Draw the feet and toes. Add sharp spikes to the tail and more plates on the back. Then add details on the body, scales, and head.

Because of the way your Stegosaurus is standing, the left hind leg does not need to be drawn. A few toes are all you see from this angle.

5 Use your felt-tip pen to trace over the pencil lines you want to keep, and erase all the others.

6 Color your Stegosaurus!

17

Witch

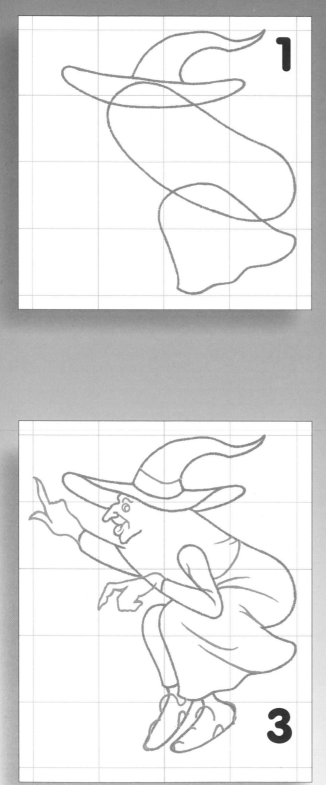

1

Draw a bean shape for the witch's body. Add the hat above and the skirt below.

2

Draw the outline of the witch's face. Add the arms, feet, and more of the skirt. Draw two curved lines across the brim of the hat.

3

Draw hands with long, pointed fingers. Add creases to the dress, and details to the face, hat, and shoes.

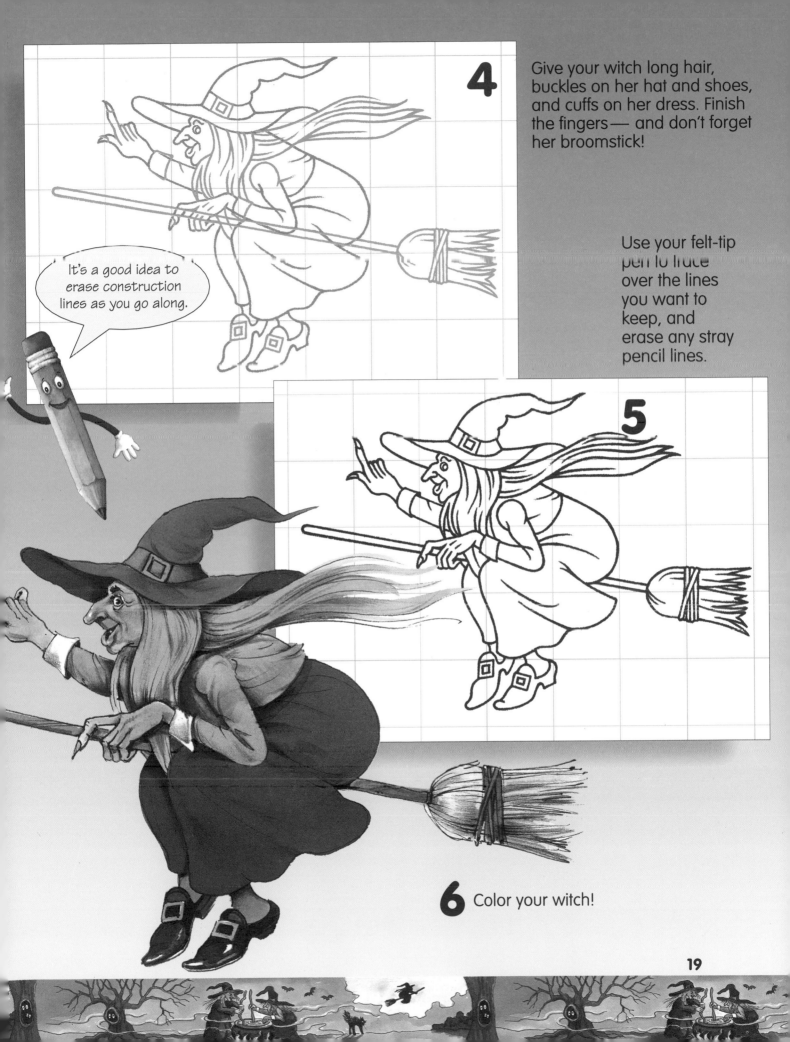

4

Give your witch long hair, buckles on her hat and shoes, and cuffs on her dress. Finish the fingers — and don't forget her broomstick!

It's a good idea to erase construction lines as you go along.

Use your felt-tip pen to trace over the lines you want to keep, and erase any stray pencil lines.

5

6 Color your witch!

19

leaves

tree

cloud

Making Backgrounds

You can add background scenery to make your pictures even more realistic. Backgrounds can add excitement that will make your drawings get noticed. Try copying the ones shown here, and then make up some of your own!

Learn to draw the Indy car on page 6. ▲

Learn to draw the Stegosaurus on page 16. ▲

Learn to draw the racoon on page 10. ▶

21

Learn to draw the giraffe on page 5. ▲

Learn to draw the bee on page 8. ▲

Helicopter

Draw the cabin, tail, stabilizer, and landing skids.

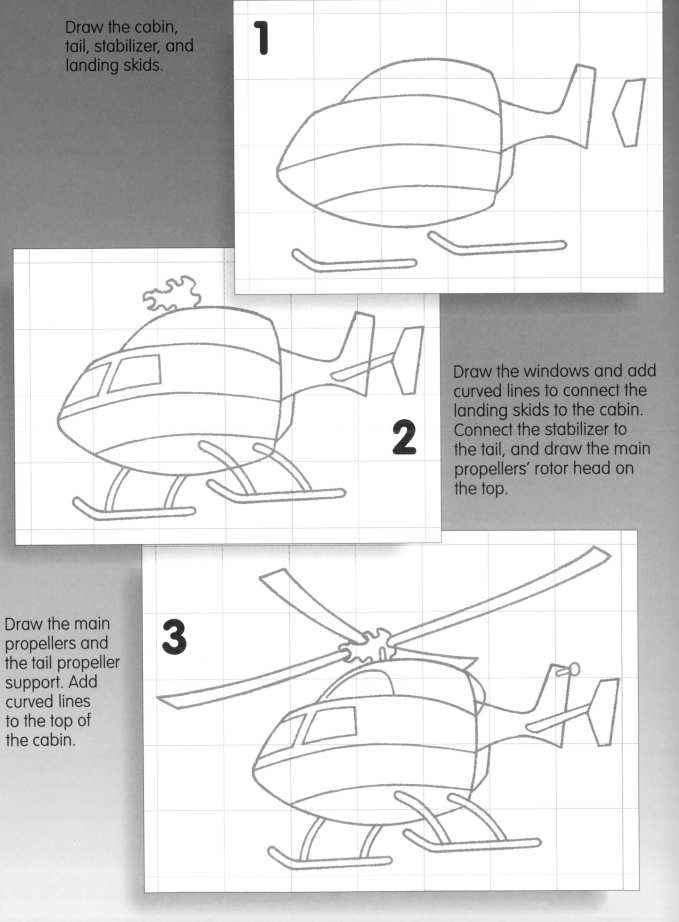

1

Draw the windows and add curved lines to connect the landing skids to the cabin. Connect the stabilizer to the tail, and draw the main propellers' rotor head on the top.

2

Draw the main propellers and the tail propeller support. Add curved lines to the top of the cabin.

3

4 Draw more windows. Add a small propeller on the tail and further details to the cabin and main propellers.

Notice how the tail propeller appears to be moving. Adding lines in the direction of the motion gives a sense of action to your drawing.

Use your felt-tip pen to trace the lines you want to keep, and erase the extra pencil lines.

5

6 Color your helicopter!

23

Purasaurolophus

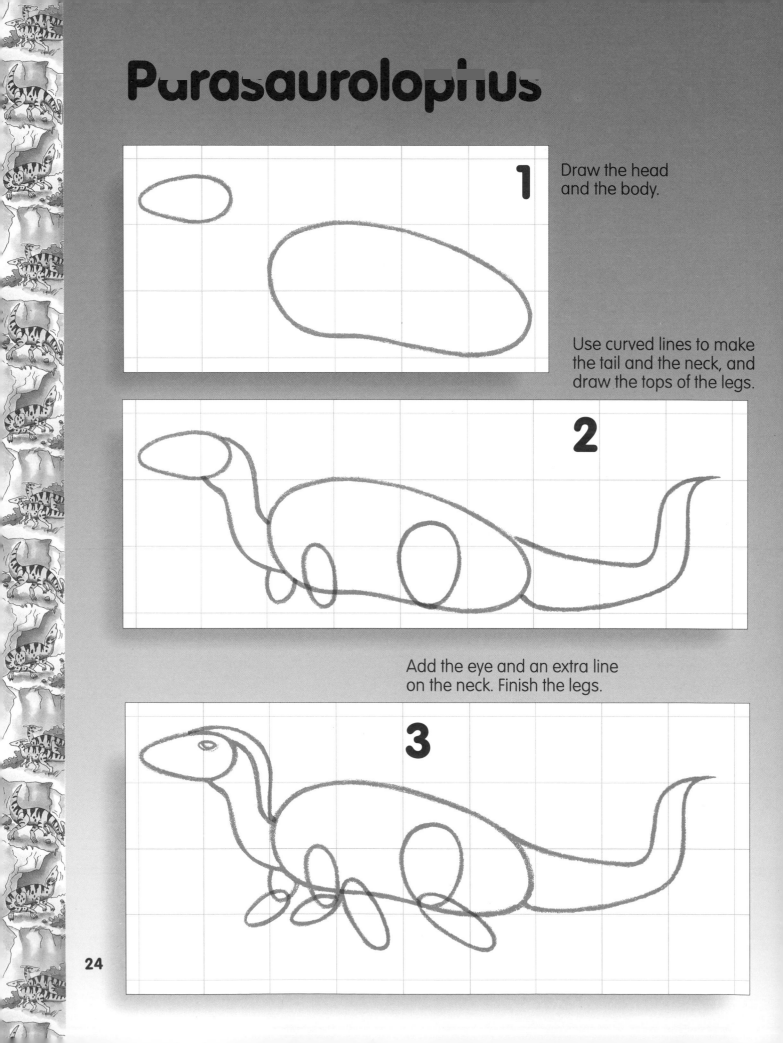

1 Draw the head and the body.

Use curved lines to make the tail and the neck, and draw the tops of the legs.

2

Add the eye and an extra line on the neck. Finish the legs.

3

4 Draw feet and claws. A long crest goes on top of this dinosaur's head. Add body markings and curved lines to define the head and body.

Use your felt-tip pen to trace over the pencil lines you want to keep, and erase all the others.

5

Try lots of colors for your Parasaurolophus!

6 Color your Parasaurolophus!

Mad Scientist

Draw the head and body.

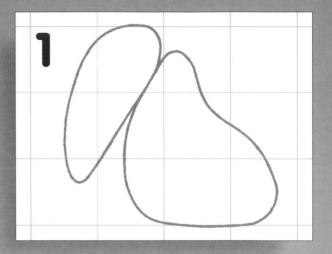

Add a long nose with two circles at the top for eyes. Draw the lab jacket.

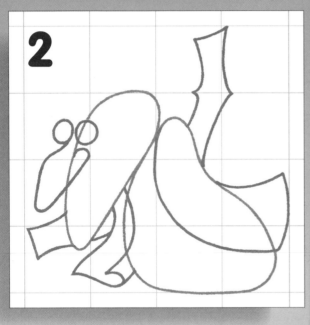

Give the scientist gnarled hands and thin legs. Draw his ear, jawline, mouth, and pupils.

26

4

Finish your drawing with hair, glasses, feet, and details on the clothing. Don't forget to give your scientist a test tube!

Use your felt-tip pen to trace over the lines you want to keep, and erase any stray pencil lines.

5

6 Color your Mad Scientist!

Terminator Alligator

Start by using curved lines to draw the alligator's torso, head, and arms.

1

2

Add the alligator's legs, hands, and facial features.

3

Give your alligator a tail and muscles on his arms, and shape his long snout. Dress him in a T-shirt and define his stomach.

Finish the feet and fingers. Give your alligator sharp teeth, eye pupils, lines across his stomach, spikes on his tail, and a barbell to hold.

4

5

Use your felt-tip pen to trace over the lines you want to keep, and erase the extra pencil lines.

6 Color your alligator!

Coloring Your Drawings

Once you've finished the outlines of your drawings, it's fun to color them in. Use watercolor paints, colored pencils, crayons, markers, or anything else you can think of!

Watercolors are fun to use, but sometimes when two wet paint colors are next to one another, they run together. If you're using watercolors, you might want to let the paint dry after each color you use.

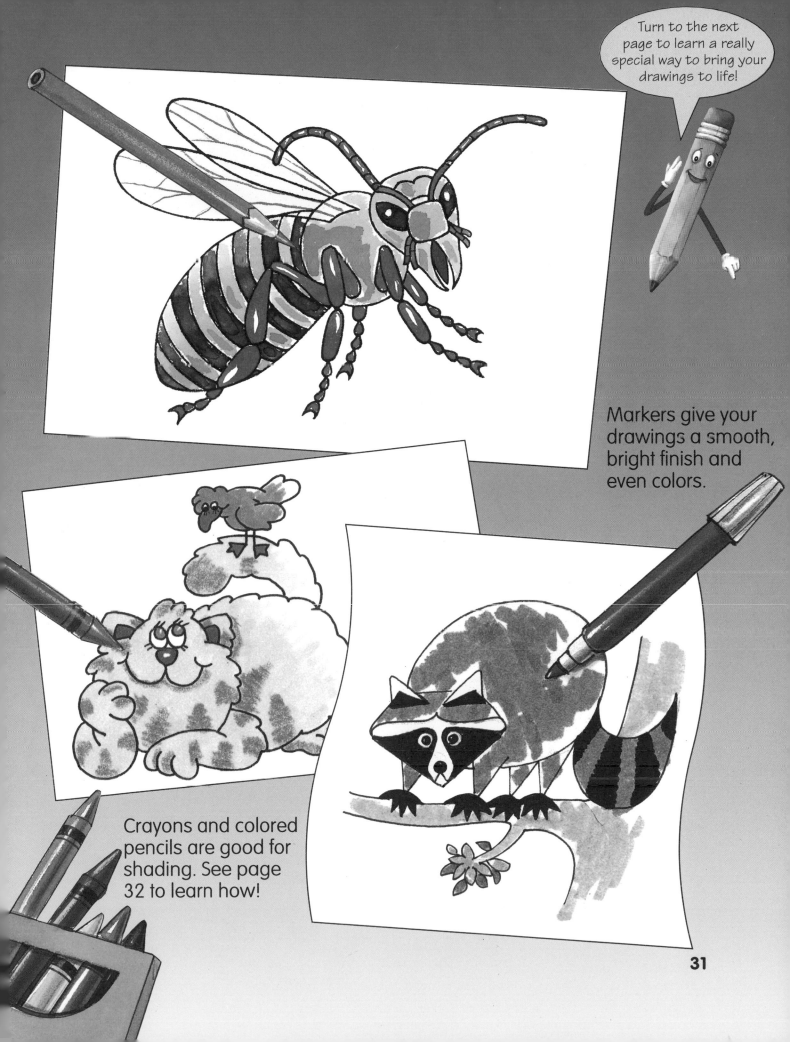

Turn to the next page to learn a really special way to bring your drawings to life!

Markers give your drawings a smooth, bright finish and even colors.

Crayons and colored pencils are good for shading. See page 32 to learn how!

Shading Your Drawings

Shading can add dimension and life to your drawings. Try shading first with a crayon or colored pencil. Make an area of your subject darker where there would be less light on the subject. Then add lighter color where the light would hit the subject and watch your drawing come to life!

Use these pull-out grid pages for your drawings. Make extra copies so you can draw lots of pictures using the steps in this book!

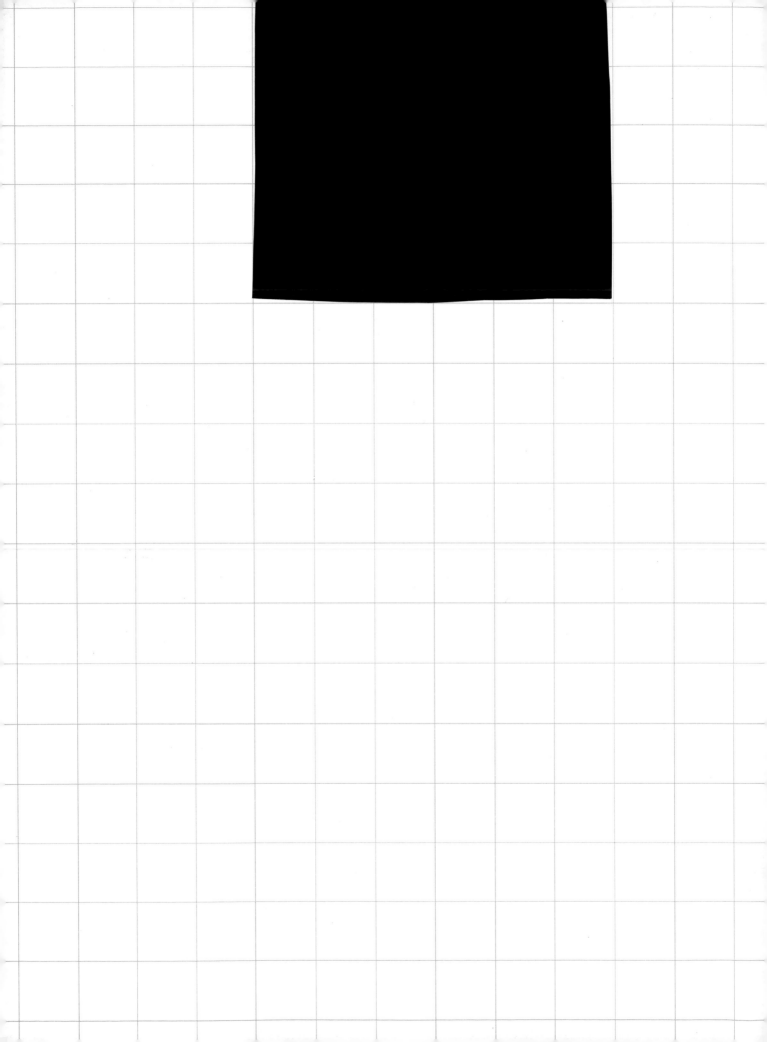